Undergraduate Writing Guide

Writing tools for the Adult Student
(APA 5th Edition)

Dr. Dean Kroeker

Outskirts Press, Inc.
Denver, Colorado

The opinions expressed in this manuscript are solely the opinions of the author and do not represent the opinions or thoughts of the publisher.

Undergraduate Writing Guide
Writing tools for the Adult Student (APA 5th Edition)
All Rights Reserved
Copyright © 2007 Dr. Dean Kroeker
V3.0

Cover Image © 2007 JupiterImages Corporation
All Rights Reserved. Used With Permission.

This book may not be reproduced, transmitted, or stored in whole or in part by any means, including graphic, electronic, or mechanical without the express written consent of the publisher except in the case of brief quotations embodied in critical articles and reviews.

Outskirts Press
http://www.outskirtspress.com

ISBN-10: 1-4327-0519-9
ISBN-13: 978-1-4327-0519-0

Outskirts Press and the "OP" logo are trademarks belonging to
Outskirts Press, Inc.

Printed in the United States of America

Foreword

Special recognition to Anna Navis, graduate student from Biola University.

Table of Contents

Introduction I
   What is APA style I
   Why do we use APA style I
   How do we use APA style II
   One final note II

Chapter One 1
Types and Elements of Papers 1
   Elements of student papers 1
      Identifying information 1
      Title 2
      Introduction 2
      Body particular to the type of paper 3
      Conclusion 4
   Elements of a writing project 4
      Preliminary pages vs. body 4
      Title page 4
      Copyright page 4
      Abstract 4
      Table of Contents 5
      Lists of Tables and Figures 5
      Reference list 5
      Appendixes 6

Chapter Two 7
Writing Style 7
   Quality of writing 7
      Keys to clear communication 8
      Plagiarism 8

Voice	8
Spelling / spell-check	8
Chapter Three	9
Formatting Style	9
Headings	9
Serrations	10
Margins	11
Pagination	11
Spacing(paragraph and page)	12
Widows and orphans	12
Font type, style, size	12
Numbers	12
Presenting statistics and data	14
Tables	15
Figures	16
Appendixes	16
Chapter Four	19
Referencing Sources	19
Quotations and In-text Citations	19
In-text quotations	19
Block quotations.	20
In-text paraphrasing and summarizing.	20
Multiple authors	21
Examples of in-text citations.	21
Reference list	22
General rules	22
Abbreviations.	23
Organization and order.	23
General forms of references.	24
Elements of a reference	25
Chapter Five	31
Specific to ResearchWriting	31
Example Reference List Entries	31
Sources of this guidebook/For more information	33
Sample Copyright Page	37
Sample Table of Contents	41
Sample Table	45
Sample Page	47
Sample Page	49
Sample Reference Page	51

Introduction

One of the overarching goals for academic writing is to ensure that students are good communicators, and that includes writing well and communicating ideas to a reader in a clear, concise, organized, consistent manner. The goals of this guidebook are conciseness, convenience and ease of use. This guidebook is based on the 5th edition of the APA manual, adapted for the adult students returning to an academic program. For ease of further reference, the specific section of the APA manual explained in each section is referenced as such: APA 5th ed., section 6.01.

What is APA style

APA writing and citation style is a standard style of writing and citations used the world over by students and professionals in multiple fields to increase effective communication. The APA first began standardizing style in 1929. The manual has been revised a number of times since then. The latest guidelines are found in:
Publication Manual of the American Psychological Association, 5th edition, Washington, DC:
   American Psychological Association, 2001.
   [Referenced in this stylebook as 'APA 5th Ed.]
The guidelines in this booklet are in compliance with 5th edition, the latest available. For complete APA guidelines, refer to the publication manual.

Why do we use APA style

Even though the APA is primarily a professional psychological organization, its guidelines are used as the standard in many disciplines. APA style is used particularly in psychology, education, and other social and behavioral sciences, such as anthropology and sociology. Other citation/publication styles include Modern Language Association (MLA), American Medical Association (AMA), Chicago, and Turabian styles. MLA is used in literature, arts, and the humanities. AMA is used in medicine, health sciences, biological sciences, and other 'hard' sciences. Chicago is the style often used in books, magazines, newspapers, and other non-scholarly publications. Turabian was designed as an adaptation of MLA and Chicago for college students to use with all subjects.

Generally, the academic discipline determines the specific standardize APA as the style used across the curriculum. The standards of APA allow for:
- Consistent rules for presentation of written content;
- Standardization of presentation format;
- Standardization of methods for organizing content; and
- Improvement of readability and communication in papers.

How do we use APA style

APA 5th ed., chapter 6

The APA manual and this guidebook, demonstrate the APA style to make their manuscript publishing guidelines appropriate for the APA style to ensure that the publishing guidelines are appropriate. This is because the APA manual is primarily geared toward formatting articles submitted for publication to APA journals (what the manual refers to as 'manuscripts'). There are slight differences in how APA treats manuscripts vs. student papers vs. multi-chapter projects. Copy manuscripts are designed to be edited and reformatted for the publication standards of the particular journal. Final manuscripts, such as course papers and projects, are submitted and evaluated accordingly. The APA even encourages adaptations of APA style when appropriate: "A number of variations from the requirements described in the *Publication Manual* are not only permissible but also desirable in the preparation of final manuscripts" (APA 5th ed., p. 322).

One final note

These guidelines are designed to allow for the standard communication of information between student and professor. Writing assignments are designed for the student to provide evidence to the professor, your mastery of a topic to the professor. APA style standardizes communication between student and professor. By writing in a uniform style, the reader(s) of your papers can give their full attention to the content of the papers, confident that they can find a source easily, if it is needed. Using the full APA style (both writing and citation), you as a writer will be communicating in a form and style that is familiar and accessible to and accepted by a broad range of professional and academic audiences.

Chapter One
Types and Elements of Papers

As a student, you will be asked to write papers in numerous categories, including summary, reflection, research, case studies, and experiential papers, among others. Your paper may present an argument for a particular thesis, or it may present research on particular information. These papers may present results of an experiment, or the results of a case study. The elements of a particular paper will be specific to the type of paper requested. Regardless, there are some elements that will appear in all papers.

Elements of student papers

All papers should have: identifying information; a title; an introduction which includes the thesis statement, hypothesis, or stated objectives; a body particular to the type of paper; and a conclusion. If any sources are cited in the text of a paper, then a Reference list must be included. The Reference list follows the body of the paper, and precedes any appendixes (see Reference list section below for details on formatting this section). Student papers are continuously paginated from beginning to end (see Pagination section below for details on this). Papers may include headings if needed for clarity and organization. If headings are used, follow the formatting guidelines below in the Headings section. A good rule of thumb for headings is to include a heading for each major point in your outline.

Identifying information

For papers without cover pages, in the upper left hand corner of the first page, on successive lines, type your full name, the assignment name, the course name, your group name, professor's name, and the date the assignment is due:

Joan Q. Student
Final Learning Paper
Organizational Ethics
Soapberry group
Dr. Scott R. Professor
December 6, 2007

For papers with title/cover pages, the same information is included: your full name, the assignment name, the course name, your group name, the professor's name, and the date the assignment is due. The title is centered left-right and top-bottom, in all caps, double-spaced and inverted-pyramid style if more than one line. The identifying information is then centered left-right at the bottom of the page:

TITLE OF PAPER, CENTERED IN ALL CAPITAL LETTERS

DOUBLE-SPACED IF MORE THAN ONE LINE

INVERTED PYRAMID STYLE

Joan Q. Student
Final Learning Paper
Organizational Ethics
Soapberry group
Dr. Paul P. Professor
December 6, 2006

In general, the default for papers is no cover page. Use a cover page for longer papers and projects whenever a professor specifies.

Title
APA 5th ed., section 1.06

The title of any paper should summarize the main idea of the paper simply and succinctly. It should concisely state the ideas, theories, and variables under discussion and the relationship between them. The APA manual offers this as a good example of a title: "Effect of Transformed Letters on Reading Speed." Avoid words that serve no useful purpose; for example, the words *method* and *results* do not normally appear in a title, nor should such phrases as *A Study of* or *An Experimental Investigation of* begin a title. Do not use abbreviations in a title; spell out all words. A title should be no longer than 10-12 words. For formatting purposes, the title of a paper is not treated as a heading.

Introduction
APA 5th ed., section 1.08

A good introduction sets the stage for a good paper, and is critical to providing your reader with basic information about your paper's content. The Introduction defines, describes, or clarifies the topic or problem addressed in the paper and places it in its historical and/or scholarly context. A good introduction briefly introduces the reader to the issue, problem, and setting. It contains no quotations. Your Introduction should include your thesis statement, hypothesis, or stated objectives. In a research study or an experimental paper, the Introduction section describes the problem, states the hypothesis, and describes the research methodology. It can also include the importance of the problem and how the study addresses the problem.

An Introduction should be one-two paragraphs, and should clearly show the reader what to expect in the rest of the paper. Introduce your problem or topic, develop the background setting to it, and then state your approach to the topic (the hypothesis, thesis statement, or stated objectives) and your rationale/expectations.

In a student paper, the Introduction section does not have a heading. Exceptions may be made in large projects, which may have multiple chapters.

Body particular to the type of paper
APA 5th ed., sections 1.09-1.12

The Body of your paper will vary depending on the type of paper assigned. Whatever your paper type, make sure the Body flows to support your thesis statement, hypothesis, or stated objectives as laid out in the Introduction. Some possibilities for Body content include: examine the facets of the topic/problem by reviewing current research and evaluate the positions held by others; analyze current data on the topic/problem; assess the interpretations of others; synthesize the information and ideas found in other people's work (Perrin, 2004, p. 28). Use headings and subheadings (formatted properly, as described below) to guide the reader through the content.

Research studies and experiments, have very defined content in the body of the paper: a literature review, method, results, and discussion (Perrin, 2004, p. 29).

A Literature Review provides a summary of scholarship (historic and current) on the paper's topic/problem. By discussing and reviewing what others have written, your topic/problem is set in its historical and scholarly context, where you can clearly see alternative perspectives and differing interpretations.

The Method section describes how the problem/topic was addressed. Labeled subsections should tell your reader who the participants were, how they were selected, what materials were used in the intervention, and what procedures were used. Typical subheadings in the Method section include: descriptions of the participants, the apparatus or materials used, and the procedure. Describe step-by-step the process by which you conducted your research.

The Results section tells what happened with your method. It summarizes and presents the information gathered by your intervention. Summarize the data collected and the statistical analysis used. This is not your raw data, but an analysis of the data presented in tables, figures, and other statistical material. If it is necessary to include raw scores or data, they can be presented in an appendix.

Evaluate and interpret the implications of your results on your hypothesis. Address how these findings related to the surveyed literature, what implications there are for future research, what alternative interpretations are available, what conclusions you have reached, and the significance of your research and results.

Conclusion

Summarize key points and main thoughts, draw connections among important ideas, and reiterate your thesis (Perrin, 2004, p. 28). No new information is presented in the Conclusion

Elements of a writing project

The basic content of a large project is the same as that of a paper described above. The main difference is that because these are longer, they are organized differently to aid in intelligibility.

Preliminary pages vs. body
APA 5th ed., section 6.02

Larger projects distinguish in formatting between introductory material and the body of the project. These preliminary pages usually include a title page, a copyright page, an abstract, a table of contents, and lists of tables and figures. They are paginated differently, and have specific formatting requirements separate from the standard formatting of body pages. (See 'Pagination' for details.)

Title page
APA 5th ed., sections 1.06, 5.15

The title page of a larger project is different than the basic title page described above. Follow the example in Appendix A to format the title page for writing a Research Proposal.

Copyright page

By including this statement with your project, you preserve your rights to the content of the project—both the research and the writing. The copyright page includes the year of publication and the author's full name, centered top-bottom and left-right. See Appendix B for an example.

Abstract
APA 5th ed., sections 1.07, 5.16, 6.02

An abstract is a brief, comprehensive summary of the contents of a paper or article; an abstract is at the professor's discretion. The abstract is the last section to be written; after all other components of the paper have been compiled. The abstract needs to be dense with information, but also readable, well-organized, brief, and self-contained. A good abstract is:

- Accurate: Ensure that your abstract correctly reflects the purpose and content of your paper. Do not include any information not appearing in the body of your paper.

- Self-contained: Define all abbreviations and acronyms that are used in your abstract. Define unique terms. Paraphrase rather than quote: your abstract should not contain any direct quotations from other sources.

- Concise and specific: Make each sentence maximally informative, especially the lead sentence. Be as brief as possible. Do not exceed 120 words. Begin the abstract with the most important information, but do not repeat the title. This may be the purpose, thesis, or perhaps the results and conclusions. Include in your abstract only the four or five most important concepts, findings, or implications.

- Non-evaluative: Report rather than evaluate. Do not add to or comment on what is in the body of your paper.

- Coherent and readable: Write in clear prose. Use the active voice, but avoid personal pronouns (I, me, my, we, our, etc.). Use third person rather than first person. Use the present tense to describe results with continuing applicability or conclusions drawn, but use the past tense to describe specific variables manipulated or tests applied.

- One paragraph which is no longer than 120 words.

The abstract is a separate page, placed after the copyright page and before the table of contents. Label the page Abstract in upper and lowercase letters, at the top of the page, centered left-right. Four lines down type the title of your paper/project, centered, all caps, double-spaced and inverted pyramid style if more than one line. Four lines down from the title type your full name. Four lines below your name begin the text of the abstract. The abstract is written as a block: double-spaced, not indented. Use the same margins as the rest of the paper. Do not exceed 120 words, and keep it one single paragraph. See Appendix C for an example of the format of an abstract.

Table of Contents

Only large projects with chapters need a table of contents (TOC). A TOC should include lists of tables and figures, if included, the chapters with their titles and any major headings in each chapter, as well as the Reference list and Appendixes. At the top of the page, type Table of Contents in upper and lowercase letters, centered left-right. The major divisions of the TOC are left-aligned: chapter titles, the reference list, and appendixes. Minor divisions are indented ½ inch (one tab).

Lists of Tables and Figures

If more than one table and/or more than one figure are used in your document, include a List of Tables and/or a List of Figures as part of your preliminary pages. See Appendix E for an example of the format of a List of Tables. A List of Figures is formatted similarly.

At the top of the page, type List of Tables in upper and lowercase letters, centered left-right. Include the table number, the title of the table, and its page number.

Chapters

Typically, the body of a large project is divided into chapters. This is for ease of writing and reading. Each chapter must include an introduction and a conclusion, in addition to the body of the chapter.

Reference list
APA 5th ed., sections 1.13, 5.18

A Reference list provides the publishing information for all sources cited in your papers. In APA style, all citations in the paper must be included in the Reference list, and all references must be cited in the text. It is a *reference* list, not a bibliography; it is a list of *works cited*, not *works consulted*. See below for comprehensive information on how to format entries in your Reference list. See

Appendix I for a sample page of a Reference list.

The reference list is a new page following the last page of text. Type the title References (Reference, in there is only one) in upper and lowercase letters, at the top of the page, centered left-right. Double-space the entire reference list: each entry is double-spaced, as well as between entries. Each reference is formatted as a hanging indent, with the first line of the reference left aligned, and subsequent lines indented ½ inch (one tab).

Appendixes
APA 5th ed., sections 1.14, 5.19, 6.02

Not all larger projects include appendixes. They are useful for detailed supplemental information that would be helpful for the reader to know, but is not necessary to include in the body of the paper, or if including the details in the body would be distracting or inappropriate. Include an appendix only if it helps readers to understand, evaluate, or replicate your study. If you do include any appendixes, they follow the Reference list at the end of the project. The following materials are more appropriate for an appendix than for in-text: original scales or questionnaires, the instrument used for data collection, raw data, statistical analysis/calculations, informed consent forms.

Appendixes are lettered, not numbered, beginning with A, in the order in which they appear in the text. Type the heading Appendix (with the appropriate identifying uppercase letter) in upper and lowercase letters, at the top of the page, centered left-right. Double-space all content in appendixes, and begin each one on a new page, lettered sequentially. If there is only one appendix, do not letter it; the title Appendix is sufficient. Two lines below the heading, type the title of the appendix, centered left-right, in upper and lowercase letters. Begin the text two lines below the appendix title. Double-space the content of the appendix.

OPTIONAL elements of papers and projects

Running header for publication
APA 5th ed., sections 1.06, 5.15

The running head is an abbreviated title that is printed at the top of the pages of a published article to identify the article for readers. The head should be a maximum of 50 characters, counting letters, punctuation, and spaces between words. The running head is often an abbreviation of the title. Unless explicitly requested by your professor, papers submitted for classes DO NOT require a running head. If your professor does request a running head as part of your paper, it should be formatted in your word processing software as part of the header, right-aligned, and preceding the page number.

Chapter Two
Writing Style

It is not just your paper's topic and content that is important to the reader. Your writing style is also critical to clearly communicating your ideas. The reader may not notice if a paper is well-written, as the style fades to allow the ideas to shine through. But a poorly-written paper distracts a reader from the ideas and focuses attention on the writing style instead of the content.

Quality of writing

It is your responsibility to produce a clean project that is free from spelling and grammatical errors. While your professors can offer guidance, they cannot be expected to function as proof readers.

Regardless of the type of paper, all papers should be written in an appropriate scholarly style and voice. Except in rare specific cases, stream-of-consciousness writing is not appropriate.

Interact with your sources. Quotes should not stand alone. Do not have one quote follow another without explanatory or connecting sentences in between. Each quote should have a sentence preceding it that leads up to and/or introduces the quote, and a sentence following it to explain the significance of the quote or to link the quote to your paragraph topic.

Make sure you have good reasoning and argumentation. The thoughts should make sense, one after another, and the paragraphs and chapters build on one another.

Make sure your grammar, word choice, and spelling are without error. Your paper should be spell-checked and proofread carefully.

If you are not a strong writer, it is better to use short, simple sentences rather than long, complex sentences.

Keys to clear communication
APA 5th ed., sections 2.01-2.04

- Orderly presentation of ideas
    - Flow of ideas, from thought units to paragraph units to outlines to sections to chapters
    - Thought development through a paragraph
    - Use punctuation and transitional words to achieve flow of thought
- Smoothness of expression
- Economy of expression
- Precision and clarity

Plagiarism
APA 5th ed., sections 6.22, 8.05

Avoiding plagiarism in your writing often begins with good research skills and techniques.

Voice

Do not use first-person or second-person pronouns (I, me, my, we, our, ours, you, your, yours), unless allowed by your professor for a specific paper. For example, research indicates that…, a study conducted by (Kroeker, 2007) states, "….

Spelling / spell-check

Be very careful of words that are spelled correctly (spell-check won't catch them), but are used incorrectly. Key words to pay attention to are: *their, there,* and *they're; to two,* and *too*; as well as *principal and principle.*

Chapter Three
Formatting Style

Headings
APA 5th ed., sections 3.30-3.32, 5.10

Headings and subheadings are used to subdivide text into logical and/or sequential sections. The APA levels of headings establish a standard format for indicating the hierarchy of sections to orient the reader to the flow of your paper. Headings function as an outline, revealing the organization of your paper.

Your headings should follow standard APA heading style, which formats five levels of headings:
CENTERED UPPERCASE HEADING (LEVEL 5)

Centered Uppercase and Lowercase Heading (Level 1)

Centered, Italicized, Uppercase and Lowercase Heading (Level 2)

Flush Left, Italicized, Uppercase and Lowercase Side Heading (Level 3)

Indented, italicized, lowercase paragraph heading ending with a period (Level 4). The text of the paragraph then begins on the same line as the heading, separated by a period and two spaces.

Only in rare cases would your writing require all five levels of headings. For example, in general, you will use Levels 1 and 3 (using Level 1 for both the chapter number and title, treating them as one heading). If you need an additional level of headings, use Level 4. Your headings for Chapter One would then look like this:

Chapter One
Statement and Description of Project

Introduction
Statement of Purpose/Thesis
The Setting
History and Background of the Situation
Scope of the Project
Importance of the Project
Conclusion

If you need…	Then use APA levels:
one level	Level 1
two levels	Levels 1 & 3
three levels	Levels 1, 3, & 4
four levels	Levels 1, 2, 3, & 4
five levels	Levels 5, 1, 2, 3, & 4

Headings flow with the text of the paper. When new headings are required, do not begin new pages. Continue the text two lines below the heading (except for Level 4, where the text begins on the same line as the heading).

Serrations
APA 5th ed., sections 3.33, 5.12

Serrations are labeling elements in a series to aid in clarity or to clarify the sequence or relationship between elements. A letter identifies elements in a series, if the series is within a sentence or paragraph, or by a number, if the series is separate paragraphs.

- Serrations within a paragraph or sentence: identify elements in a series by lowercase letters in parentheses:

    - The participant's three choices were (a) working with one other participant, (b) working with a team, and (c) working alone.

    - Participants considered (a) some alternative courses of action, (b) the factors influencing the decision, and (c) the probability of success.

- Commas separate the elements in this series, because there are no commas within each element. If there are commas within an element, then separate the elements with a semicolon:

    - We tested three groups: (a) low scorers, who scored fewer than 20 points; (b) moderate scorers, who scored between 20 and 50 points; and (c) high scorers, who scored more than 50 points.

- If the elements of a series within a paragraph constitute a compound sentence and are preceded by a colon, then capitalize the first word of the first item:

- The experiments on which we report were designed to address two such findings: (a) Only a limited class of patterned stimuli, when paired with color, subsequently contingently elicit aftereffects, and (b) decreasing the correlation between grid and color does not degrade the McCollough effect.

• Serrations which is a series of separate paragraphs: identify the elements by an Arabic numeral followed by a period but not enclosed in or followed by parentheses:

- Using the learned helplessness theory, we predicted that the depressed and non-depressed participants would make the following judgments of control:

  1. Individuals who were exposed to adverse stimuli were more likely to react negatively in subsequent situations….
  2. Non-depressed persons exposed to…
  3. Depressed persons exposed to…
  4. Depressed and non-depressed participants in the no-noise groups…

The list begins indented. The second and succeeding lines are aligned left.

In any series, with or without enumeration, any items should be syntactically and conceptually parallel to the other items in the series. Example:

Leaders are: (a) willing to take risks, (b) available to staff, and (c) considerate of different viewpoints.

Margins
APA 5th ed., sections 5.04, 6.03

The standard for margins is 1" on all sides (top, bottom, left, right). Papers are to be left-aligned, not full justified. That means that the right margin is ragged, not justified. Do not hyphenate words at the ends of lines.

For major research writing, the above rule applies, with the exception of the left margin, which is to be 1.5".

Pagination
APA 5th ed., sections 5.06, 6.02

All papers should be paginated, either in the upper right hand corner or centered at the bottom of the pages. Page numbering should be consistent through the whole paper.

Research Papers are paginated differently than other papers:
Preliminary pages (the abstract, table of contents, list of tables, list of figures, and acknowledgment/dedication pages) are paginated in lower-case Roman numerals (i, ii, iii, etc.), centered at the bottom of the page. Center the page numbers at the bottom margin, one-half inch from the bottom of the page. There is no page number on the cover page or the copyright page.

In the text, page numbers must be Arabic numbers (1, 2, 3, etc.) and must be placed at the top right corner, one-half inch from the top edge and one-half inch from the right edge. This is the default setting in most word processing software. The text must be continuously paginated, from the first page through the reference list to the end of the appendixes. You do not need a running head or a manuscript header in this paper.

That is the preferred APA page-numbering style, and is supported by most word processing software. If, however, your software program does not support this, you may number your pages as following: Beginning with the Abstract, number all pages in the upper right-hand corner, one-half inch from the top edge and one-half inch from the right edge. The cover page and copyright page do not have page numbers. Start counting pages with the Abstract as page 1.

Spacing(paragraph and page)
APA 5th ed., section 5.08

All text material must be double-spaced. Exceptions may occur in figures, tables, and other special items. Preliminary pages (title, copyright, and table of contents) follow special spacing requirements. See the appendices for examples. Do not hyphenate words at the end of a line. Indent all paragraphs 1/2 inch (one tab).

The only exceptions to this are (a) the abstract, (b) block quotations, (c) titles and headings , (d) table titles and notes, and (e) figure captions.

Widows and orphans

Avoid widows and orphans. An orphan is having one line of a paragraph or heading by itself at the bottom of the page; a widow is having one line of a paragraph left alone at the beginning of the next page. The best way to avoid this is to have your word processing software control paragraph and line placement. Microsoft Word has a widow/orphan control feature that can be activated.

Font type, style, size

The preferred font is 12 pt. Times or Times New Roman. Do not use Courier. Use a serif font (those with cross marks on individual letters). Sans serif fonts (those without cross marks) such as Arial or Century Gothic should be used to label figures and illustrations. For emphasis, use italics (*slanted type*) not underlining.

Numbers
APA 5th ed., sections 3.42-3.49

Spell out numbers under nine and any number used at the beginning of a sentence. Use Arabic numerals for numbers 10 and larger, and any number used as a percentage (%) or money ($). Use numerals for all numbers in the Abstract.

	Examples:
Numbers of 10 and larger	14 respondents, 11th article, 26 chapters
Numbers smaller than 10 when compared with numbers larger than 10 (and that appear in the same paragraph)	the 4th chapter of 20; 2 of 30 subjects; 15 sources: 3 books, 10 articles, 2 films of the 10 conditions, the 5th condition the 6th of the 12 groups;
BUT	15 traits on each of the four checklists [Traits and checklists are not being compared; they are different categories of items.]
Numbers preceding units of measurement	6 in. mark; 300-mg capsule; 12 cm wide
Numbers used statistically or mathematically: decimal quantities, percentages, ratios, percentiles, and quartiles	7.5% of respondents; a ratio of 5:2 ; 9% of the sample; the 3rd percentile; the 1st quartile; 4 times as many; multiplied by 5
Numbers that represent times	6 years; 5 months; 1 week ago; 7:15 p.m.
Numbers that represent dates	January 31, 2004; October 9, 2001
Numbers that represent ages	5-year-olds; students who are 8 years old
Numbers for population size	1.5 million citizens
Numbers that refer to participants' or subjects	7 participants; 4 rhesus monkeys
Numbers that refer to points or scores on a scale	scores of 6.5-7.0 on an 8-point scale
Numbers for exact sums of money	the cost of the test was $4.25; a $5 fee
Numbers used as numbers	a scale ranging from *1* to *5*
Numbers that indicate placement in a series	Exam 4; Figure 9
Numbers for parts of books	chapter 2; page 6
Numbers in a list of four or more numbers	The sample was composed of workgroups with 2 46 and 8 members.

But use words for numbers:	*Examples:,*
Numbers smaller than 10 (see exceptions above)	two experimental models; three lists one-topic discussion.
Zero	zero-percent increase,
Numbers that begin sentences,	Sixteen authors contributed to the project. Thirty observers approved of the project
Numbers that begin titles	"Twelve Common Errors in Research" "Seven-Point Scales: Values and Limitations"
Numbers that begin headings, including table and figure headings	Five common income groupings, Thirty Self-Identity Words
Numbers in common fractions,	two-thirds of teachers; a three-fourths reduction
Numbers in common names and phrases	the Ten Commandments; the Seven Wonders of the Ancient World; the Fourth of July

Sometimes a combination of words and numerals are used to express numbers	*Examples:*
Rounded large numbers (starting with millions)	almost 3 million people; a budget of $2.5 billion
Back-to-back modifiers	2 two-way interactions; ten 7-point scales; twenty 6-year-olds; the first 10 items

The above rules for using words vs. numerals for numbers apply whether the numbers in question are cardinal or ordinal. Cardinal numbers (one, two, three, etc.) indicate quantity; ordinal numbers (first, second, third, etc.) indicate order.

To form the plural of a number, add *s* or *es* alone, without an apostrophe. This applies to numbers both as words and numerals: threes, 1940s, 10s and 20s.

Presenting statistics and data
APA 5th ed., sections 1.10, 3.53-3.61, 5.14

Some papers will require you to present your data (either raw and/or analyzed) along with your text. Statistics, mathematical copy, raw data, and analyzed data can be presented in text, in tables, and in figures. A general rule for presenting data is:
- If you have 3 or fewer numbers to present, use a sentence;
- If you have from 4 to 20 numbers to present, use a table; and
- If you have more than 20 numbers, consider using a graph or figure instead of a table.

See below for guidelines on presenting data in tables and figures.

Tables
APA 5th ed., sections 3.62-3.74, 5.21

Use a table to present data when presenting the data in a sentence or paragraph would be too dense to comprehend. If the data is relevant to the textual discussion, then the table can be presented in the text. If the data is interesting, but not necessary to understanding the text, then present the table in an appendix. The APA manual includes a number of sample tables.

Tables are only appropriate if they are referenced in the text. An informative table supplements the text rather than duplicating it. In the text, refer to every table and tell the reader what to look for, what is notable, and why the data in and conclusions from the table are relevant. Discuss only the table's highlights, not every element. If you discuss every item of the table in text, then the table is unnecessary.

Tables are numbered with Arabic numerals (1, 2, 3, etc.) in the order in which the tables are first mentioned in the text. Use those numbers when referring to a table in the text:

As shown in Table 8, the responses were…

Children with pre-training (see Table 5)…

If tables are included in appendixes, the tables are identified with capital letters and Arabic numerals: Table A1 is the first table of Appendix A; Table C2 is the second table of Appendix C).

In addition to a table number, give every table a brief but clear explanatory title. Every column and every row needs a title as well, to identify the data under it.

To format the table, type the word Table and its Arabic numeral flush left at the top of the table. Double-space and begin the table title flush left, capitalizing the initial letters of the principal words and italicizing the title. If the title is longer than one line, double-space between lines, and begin subsequent lines flush left under the first line.

Key questions when presenting data in a table:

- Is the table necessary?
- Are the tables presented in a consistent manner?
- Are lines used effectively?
- Is the table title brief but explanatory?
- Does every column have a heading?
- Are abbreviations & special symbols explained?
- Are notes to the table ordered correctly?
- Is the table referred to in the text?
- Is the table placed appropriately within the text?

Figures
APA 5th ed., sections 3.75-3.86, 5.22

A figure may be a chart, graph, photograph, drawing, or other depiction. Consider carefully whether and when to use a figure. Tables are often preferred for the presentation of quantitative data because they provide exact information. But figures can be beneficial, as they can quickly convey an overall pattern of results.

Figures are numbered with Arabic numerals (1, 2, 3, etc.) in the order in which the figures are first mentioned in the text. Use those numbers when referring to a figure in the text:

> As shown in Figure 12, the responses were…

> Children with pre-training (see Figure 5)…

If figures are included in appendixes, the figures are identified with capital letters and Arabic numerals: Figure A1 is the first figure of Appendix A; Figure C2 is the second figure of Appendix C).

A figure includes both a legend and a caption. A legend explains the symbols used in the figure and is placed within the figure. A caption, or the title, is the figure number plus a concise explanation of the figure. It is typed below the figure.

Key questions when presenting data in a figure:

- What idea is the figure conveying?
- Is the figure necessary? If it merely duplicates text, it is not necessary. But if it complements text or eliminates lengthy discussion, then a figure may be the best way to present the information.
- What type of figure will best convey the idea? A graph, chart, diagram, drawing, map, photograph, etc.?
- Is it simple, clean, and free of extraneous detail?
- Is the figure easy to understand?
- Are the data plotted accurately?
- Is it easy to read? Is the lettering large and dark enough to read?
- Are abbreviations and symbols explained?
- Are captions descriptive and placed appropriately?
- Is the figure referred to in the text?
- Is the figure placed appropriately within the text?

Appendixes
APA 5th ed., sections 1.14, 3.90-3.93, 5.19, 6.02

An appendix allows for the inclusion of detailed information in your paper, which might be distracting to read in the main text. Common kinds of appendixes include large tables, sample questionnaires, survey instruments, raw data, and analyzed data.

If your paper has only one appendix, label it Appendix. If your paper has more than one appendix, label each one with Appendix followed by a capital letter (Appendix A, Appendix B, etc.). In your text, refer to appendixes by their labels, not their titles.

Like all parts of an APA paper, appendixes are double-spaced. Begin each one on a separate page. Type the word Appendix and the identifying capital letter (A, B, etc., in the order in which they are mentioned in the text) centered at the top of the page. Double-space and type the title of the appendix, centered, in upper and lowercase letters. Double-space, indent the first line ½ inch (one tab), and begin the text of the appendix.

Chapter Four
Referencing Sources

APA papers cite sources in two different ways: one-way for in-text references to a source, another way for the reference list at the end of the paper.

Quotations and In-text Citations
APA 5th ed., sections 3.34-3.41, 3.94-3.103, 5.13

The APA uses in-text citations instead of endnotes or footnotes. All in-text citations must include the author(s)' last name(s), the year of publication, and the relevant page number. The citation style of author-date-page number is the same, regardless of the type of source (book, chapter, article, etc.). Reference guidelines for different types of sources will differ in the Reference list (see below for details). Follow the guidelines below for information on in-text quotations (both short and long) and in-text paraphrasing or summarizing of a source.

In-text quotations

The citation is enclosed in parentheses and includes the author, the year of publication, and the abbreviations for page number ("p." for a single page and "pp." for more than one page). The period falls outside the in-text citation. For example:

"The rain in Spain falls mainly on the plain, or such was the conjecture of the medieval poet, Kroekerius Dean, who was said to have been so prolific a writer that he could compose entire sonnets while shaving" (Johnson, 1979, p. 458).

If you state the author's name as an introduction to or a part of your quotation, include the publication year after the name, and do not repeat them again in the parenthetical citation. For example:

Johnson (1979) commented, "The rain in Spain falls mainly on the plain, or such was the conjecture of the medieval poet, Kroekerius Dean, who was said to have been so prolific a writer that he could compose entire sonnets while shaving" (p. 458).

These examples are short quotations, because they contain fewer than 40 words. Short quotations are enclosed by double quotation marks. Do not have one quotation followed by another; multiple quotes must be linked by connecting and/or explanatory sentences.

Block quotations.

When a quotation contains 40 words or more, it must be set off in its own paragraph. Do not use quotation marks. Indent each line one-half inch (1/2") from the left margin, and double-space the quote. Place the period before the citation. For example:

Both the Bible and human experience make it clear that people made in the image of God have significant mental and analytical abilities.... The Bible affirms that people were made in God's image and given dominion over the rest of creation, and the exercise of dominion seems to presuppose that people are capable of rational thought and self-determination.

(Curtis, 1996, p. 77)

Limit block quotes to 40-60 words, and ensure that multiple quotes are linked with connecting and/or explanatory sentences.

In-text paraphrasing and summarizing.

At times, you may not want to directly quote a source, but merely paraphrase or summarize the source. When this is the case, you must still cite the author's name and year of publication, but the page number is not always necessary. Include the page number only if the paraphrase or summary is from one particular page of the source. For example:

Walker (2000) compared reaction times of sober and intoxicated drivers to sudden stimuli, finding that the level of intoxication was positively correlated to reaction time.

In a recent study of reaction times (Walker, 2000), intoxicated drivers reacted more slowly to sudden stimuli than did sober drivers.

If the name of the author appears as part of your sentence, as in the first example, cite only the year of publication in parentheses. Otherwise, place both the name and the year, separated by a comma, in parentheses (as in the second example).

Multiple authors

If there is more than one author of a single work, follow the following guidelines:

- When a work has **two** authors, always cite both names every time the reference occurs in your text.
- When a work has **three**, **four**, or **five** authors, cite all authors the first time the reference occurs; in subsequent citations, include only the surname of the first author, followed by 'et al.' (not italicized, and with period after 'al') and the year:
    - First citation of source:
        - Wasserstein, Zappulla, Rosen, Gerstman, and Rock (1994) found that…
    - Second citation of source:
        - Wasserstein, et al. (1994) found that…
- When a work has **six or more** authors, cite only the surname of the first author followed by 'et al' and the year. (In the reference list, however, provide the first initial and surname of the first six authors, and use 'et al.' for any remaining authors.)
- In the text, link multiple authors with the word 'and' (spelled out). In a citation and in the reference list, link multiple authors with an ampersand (&).

Examples:

As Silva and Gomez (1994) found, hurricanes are bad for Florida's economy.

"Hurricanes have a negative impact on Florida's economy" (Silva & Gomez, 1994, p. 221).

Examples of in-text citations.

Books by two authors are cited using the ampersand (&). For example:

(Hutchison & Smith, 1985, pp. 318-325).

If more than one work by the same author is cited in your project, the year will distinguish them. For example:

(Johnson, 1979, p. 458).

(Johnson, 1983, p. 210).

If more than one work by the same author published in the same year, use lowercase letters to distinguish them. Make sure that the letters are also used in your Reference list to distinguish the sources. For example:

(Johnson, 1994a, p. 221).

(Johnson, 1994b, p. 479).

If no author is listed, cite the first two or three words of the title in quotation marks. For example:

("Poetry of Spain," 1993).

Biblical references in APA style include the book, chapter, and verse, along with the translation used. Spell out the translation: 'New Living Translation' rather than 'NLT.'

Gen. 4:13 – 5:25 (New American Standard).

Job 27:1 (New International Version).

Use abbreviations for long book titles. For example:

2 Thess. 1:2 (King James Version).

Page numbers must be cited whenever a source is directly quoted, or if a paraphrase or summary comes from a specific part of a source. Your reader needs to be able to find your reference with ease. If your paraphrase or summary comes from an entire chapter, cite that as well.

(Chico & Busman, 1981, p. 332)

(Chico & Busman, 1981, chap. 3)

For electronic sources that do not have page numbers (web pages, etc.), use the paragraph number, preceded by the ¶ symbol or the abbreviation 'para.'

(Myers, 2000, ¶ 5)

(Buffman, 2004, Conclusion section, para. 1)

Reference list

The Reference list at the end of your paper has the full citation information for all your cited sources. The information in your Reference list should enable your reader to identify and retrieve your sources with ease. The Reference list includes only the sources used in your paper: if you didn't quote it or cite it, you don't include it on your Reference list. References cited in the text must appear in the Reference list, and each entry in the Reference list must be cited in the text.

General rules

- Arrange the references in alphabetical order by the author's last name or, if there is no author, by the first main word of the title. You can ignore *A*, *And*, and *The* in a title.
- Double-space all entries.
- Use hanging indent paragraph style (align the first line with the left margin, and indent all subsequent lines .5 inches from the left margin).
- Type all authors' names with the last name first, separated by a comma. Use only initials for the first and middle names, and an ampersand (&) rather than "and" before the last author's name.
- In titles of books and articles, begin only the first word of each title, subtitle, and proper

name with a capital letter. In the titles of journals, begin all significant words with a capital letter.
- Do not underline or use quotation marks around the titles of periodical articles.
- Give the full names of publishers, excluding "Co.," "Inc.," and the like.
- Use the abbreviation "p." or "pp." before page numbers in books, magazines, and newspapers, but not for scholarly journals.
- Separate each portion of each bibliography entry with a period followed by two spaces.

Abbreviations.

You may abbreviate some parts of books and other publications in your Reference list. Acceptable abbreviations include:

chap.	chapter	p.(pp.)	page (pages)
ed.	edition	Vol.	Volume (as in Vol. 4)
Rev. ed.	revised edition	vols.	Volumes (as in 4 vols.)
2nd ed.	second edition	No.	number
Ed.(Eds.)	editor, editors	Pt.	part
Trans.	translator(s)	Tech.Rep.	technical report
n.d.	no date	Suppl.	supplement

Organization and order.

Reference list entries include author(s)' last name and first/middle initials, publication year, title, and publication information. Reference lists are arranged by the first author's last name, then by publication year (if the name is the same), then by title (if the name(s) and the year are the same). The Reference list is double-spaced, and entries have a hanging indent (first line is flush with left margin, and subsequent lines are indented 1/2 inch).

Use only initials for first and middle names, and include the full surname.

Smith, J.R. (1996).

Arrange Reference list entries in alphabetical order by last name of the first author.

Adams, J.Q. (2004).

Reagan, R.W. (1996).

Multiple authors are separated by an ampersand (&).

Goodman, P. R., & Arbuckle, T. W. (1979).

When including several works by the same first author, use the following rules:
- One-author entries by the same author are arranged by year of publication, the earliest first.
  - Hewlett, L. S. (1996).
  - Hewlett, L. S. (1998).
- One-author entries precede multiple-author entries beginning with the same surname:
  - Alleyne, R. L. (2001).
  - Alleyne, R. L., & Evans, A. J. (1999).
- References with the same first author and different second or third authors are arranged alphabetically by the surname of the second author, or if the second author is the same, by the surname of the third author, and so on.
  - Gosling, J. R., Jerald, K., & Belfar, S. F. (2000).
  - Gosling, J. R., & Tevlin, D. F. (1996).
  - Hayward, D., Firsching, A., & Brown, J. (1999).
  - Hayward, D., Firsching, A., & Smigel, J. (1999).
- References with the same authors in the same order are arranged by year of publication, the earliest first.
  - Cabading, J. R., & Wright, K. (2000).
  - Cabading, J. R., & Wright, K. (2001).
- References by the same author (or by the same two or more authors in the same order) with the same publication date are arranged alphabetically by the title (excluding *A* or *The*) that follows the date. Lowercase letters—a, b, c, and so on—are placed immediately after the year, within the parentheses. When referencing/citing these sources in the text, be sure to include the letter with the year.
  - Bath, J. Q. (2001a). Control of…
  - Bath, J. Q. (2001b). Roles of…

General forms of references.

- Periodical:

Author, A. A., Author, B. B., & Author, C. C. (1996). Title of article. *Title of Periodical, xx,* xxx-

xxx.

- (where *xx* is the volume number and xxx-xxx is the page range of the article)

- Nonperiodical:

Author, A. A. (1989). *Title of work.* Location: Publisher.

- Part of a nonperiodical:

Author, A. A. (1987). Title of chapter. In A. Editor, B. Editor, & C. Editor (Eds.), *Title of book* (pp. xxx-xxx). Location: Publisher.

- Online periodical:

Author, A. A., Author, B. B., & Author, C. C. (1996). Title of article. *Title of Periodical, xx,* xxx-xxx. Retrieved month day, year, from www.onlinesource.com.

- (where www.onlinesource.com is the full link to the location of the article/source. It should not be simply the homepage of a website, if the article/item is located elsewhere. That is, the link should take your reader directly to the online location of your source, without the reader having to do a search or click through many links to sub-pages.)

- Online document:

Author, A. A. (2003). *Title of work.* Retrieved month day, year, from www.onlinesource.com.

Elements of a reference.

- Author

Examples (note the bold typeface to highlight the author element):

Kernis, M. H., Cornell, D. P., Sun, C. R., Berry, A., & Harlow, T. (1993). There's more to self-

esteem than whether it is high or low: The importance of stability of self-esteem. *Journal of*

Personality and Social Psychology, 65, 1190-1204.

Robinson, D. N. (Ed.). (1992). *Social discourse and moral judgment.* San Diego, CA: Academic

Press.

- o Invert names (surname first, then initials) for up to six authors. For seven or more co-authors, list the names of the first six, and then use 'et al.' for the rest.

- Publication date

Example (note the bold typeface to highlight the date element):

Fowers, B. J., & Olsen, D. H. **(1993)**. ENRICH Marital Satisfaction Scale: A brief research and clinical tool. *Journal of Family Psychology, 7,* 176-185.

- o If no date is available, write 'n.d.' in the parentheses where the year would be.

- Title of article or chapter

Example (note the bold typeface to highlight the title element):

Deutsch, F. M., Lussier, J. B., & Servis, L. J. (1993). Husbands at home: Predictors of paternal participation in childcare and housework. *Journal of Personality and Social Psychology, 65,* 1154-1166.

O'Neil, J. M., & Egan, J. (1992). Men's and women's gender role journeys: Metaphor for healing, transition, and transformation. In B. R. Wainrib (Ed.), *Gender issues across the life cycle* (pp. 107-123). New York: Springer.

- o Capitalize only the first word of the title and of the subtitle, if any, and any proper nouns. Do not italicize the title or place quotation marks around it.

- Title of work and publication information for periodicals

Example (note the bold typeface to highlight the title and publication elements):

Buss, D. M., & Schmitt, D. P. (1993). Sexual strategies theory: An evolutionary perspective on human mating. *Psychological Review, 100,* 204-232.

Henry, W. A., III. (1990, April 9). Beyond the melting pot. *Time, 135,* 28-31.

- o Give the periodical title in full, in uppercase and lowercase letters.
- o Give the volume number of journals, magazines, and newspapers. Do not use 'Vol.' before the number.
- o Italicize the name of the periodical and the volume number.
- o Give inclusive page numbers. Use 'pp.' only with newspapers.

- Title of work: non-periodicals

Example (note the bold typeface to highlight the title element):

Saxe, G. B. (1991). *Cultural and cognitive development: Studies in mathematical understanding.*

Hillsdale, NJ: Erlbaum.

- o Capitalize only the first word of the title and of the subtitle, if any, and any proper nouns.
- o Italicize the title.

- Title of work: part of non-periodical (book chapters)

Example (note the bold typeface to highlight the editor and title elements):

Baker, F. M., & Lightfoot, O. B. (1993). Psychiatric care of ethnic elders. In A. C. Gaw (Ed.), *Culture, ethnicity, and mental illness* (pp. 517-552). Washington, DC: American Psychiatric Press.

- o Do not invert the editor(s)' name(s); use initials, then surname.
- o For a book with two or more editors, use 'Eds.' in parentheses.

Baker, F. M., & Lightfoot, O. B. (1993). Psychiatric care of ethnic elders. In A. C. Gaw (Ed.), *Culture, ethnicity, and mental illness* (pp. 517-552). Washington, DC: American Psychiatric Press.

- o Capitalize only the first word of the title and of the subtitle, if any, and any proper nouns.
- o Italicize the title.
- o Give inclusive page numbers in parentheses after the title.

- Publication information: non-periodicals

Examples:	
US publishers:	
Location, ST:	Hillsdale, NJ:
Publisher.	Erlbaum.
Canadian publishers:	
Location,Province,Country:	Toronto, Ontario, Canada:
Publisher.	University of Toronto Press.
Non-US	non-Canadian publishers:
Location, Country:	Oxford, England:
Publisher.	Basil Blackwell.

Major publishing city:	
Major city:	Amsterdam:
Publisher.	Elsevier.

- o The Reference list must include the location of the publishers of books, reports, brochures, and other non-periodical publications (city and state for US publishers, city, province, and country for Canadian publishers, and city and country for non-US/non-Canadian publishers).

- o Use the standard two-letter postal abbreviation for US states.

- o The following cities can be listed without a state or country because they are well known for publishing:

Baltimore	New York	Amsterdam	Paris
Boston	Philadelphia	Jerusalem	Rome
Chicago	San Francisco	London	Stockholm
Los Angeles		Milan	Tokyo
		Vienna	Moscow

- Retrieval information: electronic/online sources (information here adapted from APA's updated resource on electronic references, retrieved September 17, 2004, from http://www.apastyle.org/elecmedia.html and http://www.apastyle.org/elecsource.html)

Examples:

Electronic reference formats recommended by the American Psychological Association. (2000,

October 12). Retrieved October 23, 2000, from http://www.apa.org/journals/webref.html

Brian's Story. (n.d.). Retrieved September 17, 2004, from http://www.university

name.edu/bold/profile_farr.cfm

- Direct readers as closely as possible to the information being cited; whenever possible, reference specific documents rather than home or menu pages.

- If you cannot provide a specific URL (web address) that would take the reader directly to your source, then provide as detailed/specific address as possible, and use 'available from' (rather than 'from') to indicate that the URL leads to information on how to obtain the cited material, rather than to the material itself.

- At a minimum, a reference of an Internet source should provide a document title or description, a date (either the date of publication or update or the date of retrieval), and an address (in Internet terms, a uniform resource locator, or URL). Whenever possible, identify the authors of a document as well.

- Provide addresses that work. The URL is the most critical element: If it doesn't work, readers won't be able to find the cited material, and the credibility of your paper or argument will suffer. The most common reason URLs fail is that they are transcribed or typed incorrectly; the second most common reason is that the document they point to has been moved or deleted.

- If it is an internet articles based on a print source:
  - At present, the majority of the articles retrieved from online publications are exact duplicates of those in their print versions and are unlikely to have additional analyses and data attached. This is likely to change in the future. In the meantime, the same basic primary journal reference form can be used, but if you have viewed the article only in its electronic form, you should add in brackets after the article title "Electronic version" as in the following fictitious example:

VandenBos, G., Knapp, S., & Doe, J. (2001). Role of reference elements in the selection of resources by psychology undergraduates [Electronic version]. *Journal of Bibliographic Research, 5,* 117-123.

  - If you are referencing an online article that you have reason to believe has been changed (e.g., the format differs from the print version or page numbers are not indicated) or that includes additional data or commentaries, you will need to add the date you retrieved the document and the URL.

VandenBos, G., Knapp, S., & Doe, J. (2001). Role of reference elements in the selection of resources by psychology undergraduates. *Journal of Bibliographic Research, 5,* 117-123. Retrieved October 13, 2001, from http://jbr.org/articles.html

  - If your article is from an internet-only journal:

Fredrickson, B. L. (2000, March 7). Cultivating positive emotions to optimize health and well-being. *Prevention & Treatment, 3,* Article 0001a. Retrieved November 20, 2000, from http://journals.apa.org/prevention/volume3/pre0030001a.html

  - Whenever possible, the URL should link directly to the article.

- If your source is a non-periodical document on the Internet, and is a stand-alone document, no author identified, no date:

GVU's 8th WWW user survey. (n.d.). Retrieved August 8, 2000, from

http://www.cc.gatech.edu/gvu/usersurveys/survey1997-10/

- If the author of a document is not identified, begin the reference with the title of the document.

Chapter Five
Specific to Research Writing

Example Reference List Entries

A BOOK WITH ONE AUTHOR

Zambroski, R. (1959). *Sarah Akhtar: a biography.* New York: Five Lakes Publishing.

A BOOK WITH TWO OR MORE AUTHORS

Abbar, A. & K. Hightower. (2000). *Photographic essays of the end of a century.* Atlanta: Lakes & Sons.

A BOOK WITH AN EDITOR

Chor, A. (Ed.). (1991). *Writing clearly: bullets, white space and common sense.* New York: Scootney Publishing.

A TRANSLATION OF A BOOK

Ben-Sachar, I. (1939). *Nunummy nibh.* (J. Tippett and C. Polard, trans.) Boston: Jean-Paul Deloria.

AN ANONYMOUS BOOK (NO AUTHOR)

The Chicago manual of style: fourteenth edition. (1993). Chicago: The University of Chicago Press.

A LATER EDITION OF A BOOK

Cooper, S. (1988). *Computer graphics* (new revised edition). Seattle: Litware, Inc.

A WORK IN MORE THAN ONE VOLUME

Greenberg, R. (1961). *Myth in children's* literature (Vols. 1-2). Boston: Ramona Publishing.

A SIGNED ARTICLE IN A JOURNAL

Con, A. (1984). The effect of pesticides on air quality. *Consolidated Messenger, 20,* 44-60.

A SIGNED ARTICLE IN A MONTHLY MAGAZINE

Shelly, D. B. (1994). Hardware innovations. *Awesome Computers, January 1995,* pp. 14-17.

A SIGNED ARTICLE IN A DAILY NEWSPAPER

Mughal, S. (1994, December 27). Speculation and development. *Island Hopper News*, Section D, p. 1.

AN UNSIGNED ARTICLE (NO AUTHOR)

The role of weather in economics. (1981, December 14). *Kimball Museum of Science, Quarterly Journal*, Volume IV, pp. 16-21.

A FILM OR VIDEOTAPE

Castaneda, M. A. (Supervising Director) & M. Sherman (Producer). (1937). *Mom's kitchen.* [Videotape]. Burbank, CA: School of Fine Art.

COMPUTER SOFTWARE

Microsoft Office (1987-2002). [Computer program]. Redmond, WA: Microsoft.

Sources of this guidebook/For more information

Writing help:
John Sheridan Biays and Carol Wershoven, *Along these Lines: Writing Paragraphs and Essays*, 3rd edition, Upper Saddle River (NJ): Pearson/Prentice Hall, 2004.

APA help:
Robert Perrin, *Pocket Guide to APA Style*, Boston: Houghton Mifflin, 2004

www.apastyle.org

Appendix A

TITLE OF RESEARCH PAPER, CENTERED AND IN ALL CAPITAL LETTERS

DOUBLE-SPACED IF MORE THAN ONE LINE

INVERTED PYRAMID STYLE

―――――――

A Research Proposal

Presented to

The Faculty of the

School of Professional Studies

Adult Program

University Name

―――――――

In Partial Fulfillment

of the Requirements for the Degree of

Bachelor of Science

―――――――

by

John Doe Smith
December 2007

Appendix B

Sample Copyright Page

Copyright © 2007 by John Doe Smith

Appendix C

Sample Abstract

Abstract

TITLE OF RESEARCH PROPOSAL, CENTERED AND IN ALL CAPITAL LETTERS

DOUBLE-SPACED IF MORE THAN ONE LINE

INVERTED PYRAMID STYLE

John Doe Smith

Four lines below the name begin the text of the abstract. The abstract is written as a block: double-spaced, not indented. Use the same margins as the rest of the paper. The abstract is a summary of the essential points and findings of the papers and not an introduction or a mere list of topics. Do not exceed 120 words, and keep it one single paragraph. Your abstract should be the last thing you write, after you have completed your entire project.

Appendix D

Sample Table of Contents

Table of Contents   Page

Chapter One: Statement and Description of the Problem 1

Introduction1

Statement of Purpose 2

Problem/Thesis Statement 2

Hypothesis 2

The Setting….. 3

History and Background of the Situation 4

   Scope of the Project 9

   Importance of the Project 15

   Conclusion…. 17

Chapter Two: Survey Literature 18

Chapter Three: Intervention Plan 35

Chapter Four: Evaluation, Methodology, and Results 42

Chapter Five: Conclusions and Recommendations 48

References 56

Appendixes 58

Appendix E

Sample List of Tables

The list of tables follows the table of contents, at the beginning of the project.

List of Tables

Page

1. Sources of Income and Expenditure.   25

2. Time Allocation in Hours and Percentage of Total Hours in Each Academic Discipline Area   30

Appendix F

Sample Table

Table 1

<u>Epistemological Classification</u>

<u>Instrumentalist</u>	<u>Critical Realist</u>	<u>Naive Realist</u>
Open	Guarded	Closed
Relative	Absolute/Relative	Absolute
Phenomenalist	Critical Empiricist	Reductionist
Culturally Specific	Incorporate	Universal
Inductive	Coherent	Deductive
Unity	Creative Tension	Conflict

<u>Note</u>: From Smith (1990, p. 10).

Begin the table two inches from the top of the page. Type "Table [#]" at the left margin.

Two lines below type the title of the table. Center the title and capitalize the first letter of each major word. Underline the title. Double-space between lines if the title is more than one line.

Four lines below the title begin the text of the table. Capitalize the first letter of each major word in headings within the table. Underline headings.

Appendix G

Sample Page

The following has a good mix of block quotes with briefer quotes.

God wants us to be knowledgeable about the assets He has entrusted to us. "Be sure you know the condition of your flocks, give careful attention to your herd…" (Prov. 27:23, New International Version). For herds or flocks, substitute what one actually has. Frank E. Gaebelein (1991), editor of *The Expositor's Bible Commentary on the Book of Proverbs*, gives his explanation of Proverbs 27:23-24: People should preserve what income they have, because it does not endure long. The main instruction is to take care of your livelihood. The motivation for this is that riches do not last long (p. 1101).

Principle Two: Financial Freedom Requires Planning

In reference to the second biblical principle (planning), the apostle Paul states in 1 Cor. 14:40, "Let all things be done decently and in order" (King James Version). Webster's Dictionary refers to order as "a definite plan" (Guralnik, 1987, p. 422). Decently (*euschemonos*) means, "everything is to be done properly and in good order." Order (*taxin*) carries a similar meaning: "in an orderly manner" (Metz, 1968, p. 455). God is a God of order and peace. His blessing rests upon those who live "properly and in an orderly manner" (Burkett, 1991, p. 55).

Larry Burkett (1991) gives his comments on planning:

God is an orderly provider. The physical world is not chaotic but orderly and well planned. Atoms stay together because God so ordered them. Finances are another aspect of the Christian's life that God wants to manage. If we are stewards and God is the owner, we must seek His wisdom. Therefore, we must go to God's Word for our plans. (p. 7)

Appendix H

Sample Page

CHAPTER 5

EVALUATION, METHODOLOGY, AND RESULTS

A five-point, Likert-style questionnaire will be the focal point of the evaluation design in Objective 1 (helping pastoral staff understand the need for discipline regarding personal finances), that will then show the need for Objective 2. When the established personal financial program has begun, the research will focus on measuring the participants' financial status.

The target population will be Florence Avenue Foursquare Church, a church with approximately 2,000 members. The scope and sample population of the research will be adults (18 years of age and up) in attendance at the first and second Sunday morning services. In the first service, there will be approximately 400 in attendance, and approximately 360 (90%) will be adults. In the second service, there will be approximately 1,000 in attendance, and approximately 900 (90%) will be adults.

Objective 1: To Help Pastoral Staff Understand the Need for Discipline Regarding Personal Finances.

Sporadic PowerPoint presentations on statistics about personal financial debt will be shown for a few weeks. Then, to measure each adult's personal financial condition, a five-point, Likert-style questionnaire will be handed out to both congregations. The questionnaire will focus on issues like basic budgeting, using a checkbook, and recognizing the warning signs of impending financial doom (see Appendix A).

Appendix J

Sample Reference Page

References

Merrill, B. (2001). Learning and teaching in universities: Perspectives from adult learners and lecturers. *Teaching in Higher Education, 6,* 5-13.

Mezirow, J. (1985). A critical theory of self-directed learning, *New Directions for Continuing Education, 25,* 35-43.

Michalski, W. J. (1986). Assessment of an off-campus Bachelor of Arts in management program. (Doctoral Dissertation, Pepperdine University, Malibu, 1986). *Dissertation Abstracts International,* 47 (11), 3945A.

Moustakas, C. (1994). *Phenomenological research methods.* Thousand Oaks, CA: Sage Publications.

Nah, Y. (1999). Can a self-directed learner be independent, autonomous, and interdependent: Implications for practice. *Adult Learning, 11* (1), 18-21.

Okech, J. (1997). Pedagogy in teaching at the university. *Journal of Instructional Psychology, 24,* 108-111.

Patterson, W. (2000). Grounding school culture to enable real change. *Education Digest, 65* (9), 4-5.

Printed in the United States
135180LV00001B/99/A